© Safoo Publications 2020

Written and illustrated by Amal Al-Aride

All rights reserved. No part of this publication may be reproduced, distributed, or transmitted in any form or by any means, including photocopying, recording, or other electronic or mechanical methods, without the prior written permission of the publisher.

Preface
(for parents)

The Nahj al-Balagha (Peak of Eloquence) is a famous collection of sermons, letters, tafsirs and narrations attributed to Imam Ali (peace be upon him), cousin and son-in-law of the Holy Prophet Muhammad (peace be upon him and his family). It was collected by Ash-Sharif Ar-Radhi, a scholar from the 10th century CE (4th century AH). Nahjul Balagha is known for its eloquent content.

'Nahjul Balagha Made Easy' is here to help you
and your child (4+ years) on the journey of understanding the Islam.

Do remember this book is not a translation, it is adapted text from a from a range of 10 Sermons selected for a your little ones.

Have plenty of fun with these wonderful collections and we hope In'sha'Allah your child has the best start in life when it comes to their faith.

Nahjul Balagha
Made Easy

Safoo Publications

Sermon 185: Allah (swt)

Allah is amazing, we cannot see him
Subhana wata'alah
The Amazing!
with our eyes and we cannot imagine
Him with our minds.
He is real and that is true because he
made us and unlike everything else, there

is only one Allah and there is
nothing like him. Allah is honest and
everything he says is true. Allah treats us

all fairly, He created us and there is
no escape when meeting Allah as all of us
will meet him one day.

Praise be to Allah. He is such that senses cannot perceive Him, place cannot contain Him, eyes cannot see Him and veils cannot cover Him. He proves His eternity by the coming into existence of His creation, and (also) by originating His creation (He proves) His existence, and by their (mutual) similarity He proves that there is nothing similar to Him. He is true in His promise. He is too high to be unjust to His creatures. He stands by equity among His creation and practices justice over them in His commands. He provides evidence through the creation of things of His being from ever, through their marks of incapability of His power, and through their powerlessness against death of His eternity.

الْحَمْدُ للهِ الَّذي لاَ تُدْرِكُهُ الشَّوَاهِدُ، وَلاَ تَحْوِيهِ الْمَشَاهِدُ، وَلاَ تَرَاهُ النَّوَاظِرُ، وَلاَ تَحْجُبُهُ السَّوَاتِرُ، الدَّالِّ عَلَى قِدَمِهِ بِحُدُوثِ خَلْقِهِ، وَبِحُدُوثِ خَلْقِهِ عَلَى وجُودِهِ، وَبِاشْتِبَاهِهِمْ عَلَى أَنْ لاَ شَبَهَ لَهُ، الَّذِي صَدَقَ في مِيعَادِهِ، وَارْتَفَعَ عَنْ ظُلْمِ عِبَادِهِ، وَقَامَ بِالْقِسطِ فِي خَلْقِهِ، وَعَدَلَ عَلَيْهِمْ فِي حُكْمِهِ، مُسْتَشْهِدٌ بِحُدُوثِ الأَشْيَاءِ عَلَى أَزَلِيَّتِهِ، وَبِمَا وَسَمَهَا بِهِ مِنَ الْعَجْزِ عَلَى قُدْرَتِهِ، وَبِمَا اضْطَرَّهَا إِلَيْهِ مِنَ الْفَنَاءِ عَلَى دَوَامِهِ،

Sermon 185: The Holy Prophet
(peace be upon him and his family)

The Holy Prophet Muhammad

(peace be upon him)

only does what Allah *Subhana wata'alah The Amazing!* says. Allah chose the Holy Prophet and his **family** to let everyone know about Islam. Allah sent the Prophet as a **teacher** to make sure that everyone knew about Allah and what He wants from us. The Holy Prophet taught people how to do things the right way and how Muslims should behave. All the **wonderful** things about Islam was kept alive by Allah and the Holy Prophet.

Zakat

I stand witness that Muhammad is His slave. His chosen Prophet and His responsible trustee –– may Allah bless him and his descendants. Allah sent him with undeniable proofs, a clear success and open paths. So he conveyed the message declaring the truth with it. He led the people on the (correct) highway, established signs of guidance and minarets of light, and made Islam's ropes strong and its knots firm.

وَأَشْهَدُ أَنَّ مُحَمَّداً عَبْدُهُ الصَّفِيُّ، وَأَمِينُهُ الرَّضِيُّ (صلى الله عليه وآله وسلم) أَرْسَلَهُ بِوُجُوبِ الْحُجَجِ، وَظُهُورِ الْفَلَجِ، وَإِيضَاحِ الْمَنْهَجِ، فَبَلَّغُ الرِّسَالَةَ صَادِعاً بِهَا، وَحَمَلَ عَلَى الْمَحَجَّةِ دالاً عَلَيْهَا، وَأَقَامَ أَعْلامَ الأَهْتِدَاءِ وَمَنَارَ الضِّيَاءِ، وَجَعَلَ أَمْرَاسَ الأَسْلامِ مَتِينَةً، وَعُرَا الأَيمَانِ وَثِيقَةً.

Sermon 185: The Ant

Have you ever thought about the really tiny things in the world that Allah has created? *Subhana wata'alah The Amazing!*

Even though the ants which Allah created are so **tiny and delicate**, they have bones, skin and eyes and ants can leap, carry its food and build its home in the ground by making tiny little holes. Ants collect food during the summer, so they have enough for winter. They are so **smart** that they make plans for their future, this is so they can stay alive. Allah is so kind, He made sure that even the **tiniest** ant could look after itself.

Do they not see the small things He has created, how He strengthened their system and opened for them hearing and sight and made for them bones and skins? Look at the ant with its small body and delicate form. It can hardly be seen in the corner of the eye, nor by the perception of the imagination – how it moves on the earth and leaps at its livelihood. It carries the grain to its hole and deposits it in its place of stay. It collects during the summer for its winter, and during strength for the period of its weakness. Its livelihood is guaranteed, and it is fed according to fitness. Allah, the Kind, does not forget it and (Allah the Giver) does not deprive it, even though it may be in dry stone or fixed rocks.

وَلَوْ فَكَّرُوا فِي عَظِيمِ الْقُدْرَةِ، وَجَسِيمِ النِّعْمَةِ، لَرَجَعُوا إِلَى الطَّرِيقِ، وَخَافُوا عَذَابَ الْحَرِيقِ، وَلَكِنَّ الْقُلُوبَ عَلِيلَةٌ، وَالْأَبْصَارَ مَدْخُولَةٌ! أَلاَ تَنْظُرُونَ إِلَى صَغِيرِ مَا خَلَقَ اللهُ، كَيْفَ أَحْكَمَ خَلْقَهُ، وَأَتْقَنَ تَرْكِيبَهُ، وَفَلَقَ لَهُ السَّمْعَ وَالْبَصَرَ، وَسَوَّى لَهُ الْعَظْمَ وَالْبَشَرَ. انْظُرُوا إِلَى النَّمْلَةِ فِي صِغَرِ جُثَّتِهَا، وَلَطَافَةِ هَيْئَتِهَا، لاَ تَكَادُ تُنَالُ بِلَحْظِ الْبَصَرِ، وَلاَ بِمُسْتَدْرَكِ الْفِكَرِ، كَيْفَ دَبَّتْ عَلَى أَرْضِهَا، وَصَبَّتْ عَلَى رِزْقِهَا، تَنْقُلُ الْحَبَّةَ إِلَى جُحْرِهَا، وَتُعِدُّهَا فِي مُسْتَقَرِّهَا. تَجْمَعُ فِي حَرِّهَا لِبَرْدِهَا، وَفِي وُرُودِهَا لِصَدَرِهَا، مَكْفُولٌ بِرِزْقِهَا، مَرْزُوقَةٌ بِوِفْقِهَا، لاَ يُغْفِلُهَا الْمَنَّانُ، وَلاَ يَحْرِمُهَا الدَّيَّانُ، وَلَوْ فِي الصَّفَا الْيَابِسِ، وَالْحَجَرِ الْجَامِسِ

Sermon 185: Allah Created Everything

Subhana wata'alah
The Amazing!

Allah made everything and he did this all alone. He had no help. If you think about it enough, you will come to see that Allah made everything, He made ants which are so small and palm trees which are so tall. Even though both of these living things are so different, He made them. They are different but also similar in some ways, both are living things, with lots of different details, textures and colours to them. Allah created everything, big, small, heavy, light, strong and weak, all these things have similarities.

No other originator took part with Him in its origination and no one having power assisted Him in its creation. If you tread on the paths of your imagination and reach its extremity it will not lead you anywhere except that the Originator of the ant is the same as He who is the Originator of the date-palm, because everything has (the same) delicacy and detail, and every living being has little difference. In His creation, the big, the delicate, the heavy, the light, the strong, the weak are all equal.

وَلَوْ فَكَّرْتَ فِي مَجَارِي أُكُلِهَا، وَفِي عُلُوهَا وَسُفْلِهَا، وَمَا فِي الْجَوْفِ مِنْ شَرَاسِيفِ بَطْنِهَا، وَمَا فِي الرَّأْسِ مِنْ عَيْنِهَا وَأُذُنِهَا، لَقَضَيْتَ مِنْ خَلْقِهَا عَجَباً، وَلَقِيتَ مِنْ وَصْفِهَا تَعَبا. فَتَعَالَى الَّذِي أَقَامَهَا عَلَى قَوَائِمِهَا، وَبَنَاهَا عَلَى دَعَائِمِهَا. لَمْ يَشْرَكْهُ فِي فِطْرَتِهَا فَاطِرٌ، وَلَمْ يُعِنْهُ عَلَى خَلْقِهَا قَادِرٌ. وَلَوْ ضَرَبْتَ فِي مَذَاهِبِ فِكْرِكَ لِتَبْلُغَ غَايَاتِهِ، مَا دَلَّتْكَ الدَّلاَلَةُ إِلاَّ عَلَى أَنَّ فَاطِرَ النَّمْلَةِ هُوَ فَاطِرُ النَّخْلَةِ، لِدَقِيقِ تَفْصِيلِ كُلّ شَيْء، وَغَامِضِ اخْتِلاَفِ كُلّ حَيّ، وَمَا الْجَلِيلُ وَاللَّطِيفُ، وَالثَّقِيلُ وَالْخَفِيفُ، وَالْقَوِيُّ وَالضَّعِيفُ، فِي خَلْقِهِ إِلاَّ سَوَاءٌ.

Sermon 185: The Creation of the Universe

Look at the way **Allah** *Subhana wata'alah The Amazing!* made the sky, the wind, the air we breath and water. How He made the sun, the moon, the **plants** and the **trees**. The way He made day and night work together, and the way **seas** flow, and the mountains that are so high. All work together, so that people like us, from different parts of the world, who speak different **languages** have a **wonderful** place to live. It should be easy to understand and see, when we take a look at all these wonderful things, that Allah is real and He made **everything.**

So is (the creation of) the sky, the air, the winds and the water. Therefore, you look at the sun and moon, the plants and trees, water and stone, the alternation of this night and day, the flowing out of these seas, the large number of mountains and the height of their peaks, the diversity of languages and the variety of tongues. Then woe be to him who disbelieves in the Ordainer and denies the Ruler. They claim that they are like grass for which there is no cultivator nor any maker for their diverse shapes. They have not relied on any argument for what they assert, nor on any research for what they have heard. Can there be any construction without a Constructor, or any offence without an offender.

وَكَذلِكَ السَّماءُ وَالْهَوَاءُ، وَالرِّيَاحُ وَالْمَاءُ. فَانْظُرْ إِلَى الشَّمْسِ وَالْقَمَرِ، وَالنَّبَاتِ وَالشَّجَرِ، وَالْمَاءِ وَالْحَجَرِ، وَاخْتِلَافِ هذَا اللَّيْلِ وَالنَّهَارِ، وَتَفَجُّرِ هذِهِ الْبِحَارِ، وَكَثْرَةِ هذِهِ الْجِبَالِ، وَطُولِ هذِهِ الْقِلَالِ، وَتَفَرُّقِ هذِهِ اللُّغَاتِ، وَالْأَلْسُنِ الْمُخْتَلِفَاتِ. فَالوَيْلُ لِمَنْ جَحَدَ الْمُقَدِّرَ، وَأَنْكَرَ الْمُدَبِّرَ. زَعَمُوا أَنَّهُمْ كَالنَّبَاتِ مَا لَهُمْ زَارِعٌ، وَلَا لِاخْتِلَافِ صُوَرِهِمْ صَانِعٌ، وَلَمْ يَلْجَأُوا إِلَى حُجَّةٍ فِيَما ادَّعَوْا، وَلَا تَحْقِيقٍ لِمَا أَوْعَوْا، وَهَلْ يَكُونُ بِنَاءٌ مِنْ غَيْرِ بَانٍ، أَوْ جِنَايَةٌ مِن غَيْرِ جَانٍ

Sermon 185: The Locust

Subhana wata'alah
The Amazing!

Allah made Locusts, they are insects with two red eyes with small ears, a mouth, with two teeth to cut with two thin legs to grip things with. Allah also

made them **smart, quick** and sensitive to their environment, so they can feel what's around them. Even

though they are **so little** and as thin

as a **finger**, farmer's are scared of them because locusts gather with their

friends and like to **eat** all the farmer's crops when they are hungry.

If you wish you can reflect on the locust (as well). Allah gave it two red eyes, lighted for them two moon-like pupils, made for it small ears, opened for it a suitable mouth and gave it keen sense, gave it two teeth to cut with and two sickle-like feet to grip with. The farmers are afraid of it in the matter of their crops since they cannot drive it away even though they may join together. The locust attacks the fields and satisfies its desires (of hunger) from them although its body is not equal to a thin finger.

وَإِنْ شِئْتَ قُلْتَ فِي الْجَرَادَةِ، إِذْ خَلَقَ لَهَا عَيْنَيْنِ حَمْرَ اوَيْنِ،
وَأَسْرَجَ لَهَا حَدَقَتَيْنِ قَمْرَاوَيْنِ، وَجَعَلَ لَهَا السَّمْعَ الْخَفِيَّ، وَفَتَحَ لَهَا
الْفَمَ السَّوِيَّ، وَجَعَلَ لَهَا الْحِسَّ الْقَوِيَّ، وَنَابَيْنِ بِهِمَا تَقْرِضُ،
وَمِنْجَلَيْنِ بِهِمَا تَقْبِضُ، يَرْهَبُهَا الزُّرَّاعُ فِي زَرْعِهِمْ، وَلاَ
يَسْتَطِيعُونَ ذَبَّهَا، وَلَوْ أَجْلَبُوا بِجَمْعِهِمْ، حَتَّى تَرِدَ الْحَرْثَ فِي
نَزَوَاتِهَا، وَتَقْضِي مِنْهُ شَهَوَاتِهَا، وَخَلْقُهَا كُلُّهُ لاَ يُكَوِّنُ إِصْبَعاً
مُسْتَدِقَّةً.

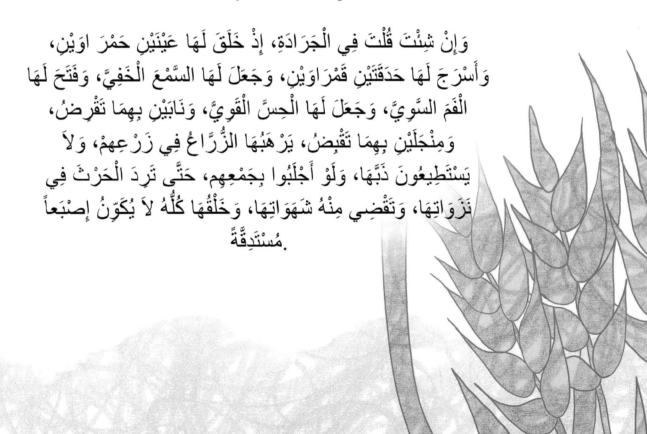

Sermon 185: Birds

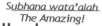

Subhana wata'alah
The Amazing!

Allah made birds and they do what He tells them to. Allah knows **everything** about His creation. He knows the amount of **feathers** on all the birds that he has made. He made their **feet** so that they could stand and He created them so that they can look after themselves. He **knows** them all because He created them. He made crows, eagles pigeons and ostriches. He made the clouds and **rain** so that the earth could grow trees and **plants** so all of Allah's creatures have food.

The birds are bound by His commands. He knows the number of their feathers and their breaths. He has made their feet to stand on water and on land. He has ordained their livelihoods. He knows their species: this is the crow, this is the eagle, this is the pigeon and this is the ostrich. He called out every bird with its name (while creating it) and provided it with it's livelihood. He created "..heavy clouds" (13:12) and produced from them heavy rain and spread it on various lands. He drenched the earth after its dryness and grew vegetation from it after its barrenness.

فَتَبَارَكَ اللهُ الَّذِي يَسْجُدُ لَهُ (مَنْ فِي السَّماوَاتِ وَالأرْضِ طَوْعاً وَكَرْهاً)، وَيُعَفِّرُ لَهُ خَدّاً وَوَجْهاً، وَيُلْقِي بِالطَّاعَةِ إِلَيْهِ سِلْماً وَضَعْفاً، وَيُعْطِي الْقِيَادَ رَهْبَةً وَخَوْفاً. فَالطَّيْرُ مُسَخَّرَةٌ لِأَمْرِهِ، أَحْصَى عَدَدَ الرِّيشِ مِنْهَا وَالنَّفَسَ، وَأَرْسَى قَوَائِمَهَا عَلَى النَّدَى وَالْيَبَسِ، قَدَّرَ أَقْوَاتَهَا، وَأَحْصَى أَجْنَاسَهَا، فَهذَا غُرَابٌ وَهذَا عُقَابٌ، وَهذَا حَمَامٌ وَهذَا نَعَامٌ، دَعَا كُلَّ طَائِرٍ بِاسْمِهِ، وَكَفَلَ لَهُ بِرِزْقِهِ. وَأَنْشَأَ (السَّحَابَ الثِّقَالَ)، فَأَهْطَلَ دِيَمَهَا، وَعَدَّدَ قِسَمَهَا، فَبَلَّ الأَرْضَ بَعْدَ جُفُوفِهَا، وَأَخْرَجَ نَبْتَهَا بَعْدَ جُدُوبِهَا.

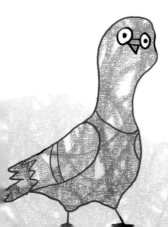

Sermon 186: Allah (swt)

Subhana wata'alah
The Amazing!

Allah,

He is not affected by time, nothing helps Him and nothing can stop Him. He has no beginning and He has no end. He has no eyes but he sees all, He has no ears but He hears all, He has no mind but He knows all. There is nothing similar to Him and there is nothing opposite to Him. He made all things similar and opposite, He made darkness and light, He made dryness and moisture and the heat and the cold.

Times do not keep company with Him, and implements do not help Him. His Being precedes times. His Existence precedes non-existence and His eternity precedes beginning. By His creating the senses it is known that He has no senses. By the contraries in various matters it is known that He has no contrary, and by the similarity between things it is known that there is nothing similar to Him. He has made light the contrary of darkness, brightness that of gloom, dryness that of moisture and heat that of cold.

لاَ تَصْحَبُهُ الأَوْقَاتُ، وَلاَ تَرْفِدُهُ الأَدَوَاتُ، سَبَقَ الأَوْقَاتَ كَوْنُهُ، وَالْعَدَمَ وُجُودُهُ، وَالابْتِدَاءَ أَزَلُهُ. بِتَشْعِيرِهِ الْمَشَاعِرَ عُرِفَ أَنْ لاَ مَشْعَرَ لَهُ، وَبِمُضَادَّتِهِ بَيْنَ الأُمُورِ عُرِفَ أَنْ لاَ ضِدَّ لَهُ، وَبِمُقَارَنَتِهِ بَيْنَ الأَشْيَاءِ عُرِفَ أَنْ لاَ قَرِينَ لَهُ. ضَادَّ النُّورَ بِالظُّلْمَةِ، وَالْوُضُوحَ بِالْبُهْمَةِ، وَالْجُمُودَ بِالْبَلَلِ، وَالْحَرُورَ بِالصَّرَدِ

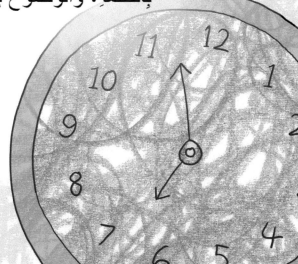

Sermon 192: Satan

Iblees (Satan) is terrible and he doesn't like Allah *Subhana wata'alah* *The Amazing!* and he **hates** us too. He is bad and he does **bad things** and tries to encourage us to do bad things with **whispers**. He tries to catch us with his bow and arrow, which he aims for us.

In the Holy **Quran**, Iblees says, "I try my very hardest to make all the people in the **world** do bad things, I will encourage them to make **mistakes** just like I have done."

Therefore, you should fear lest the enemy of Allah, (Satan) infects you with his disease, or 'leads you astray through his call, or marches on you with his horsemen and footmen', (ref. 17:64) because, by my life, he has put the menacing arrow in the bow for you, has stretched the bow strongly, and has aimed at you from a nearby position, and He (Satan) said: "My Lord! Because Thou hast left me to stray, certainly will I adorn unto them the path of error, and certainly will I cause them all to go astray." (Quran, 15:39)

فَاحْذَرُوا عَدُوَّ اللهِ أَنْ يُعْدِيَكُمْ بِدَائِهِ، وَأَنْ يَسْتَفِزَّكُمْ [بِنِدَائِهِ، وَأَنْ يُجْلِبَ عَلَيْكُمْ] بِخَيْلِهِ وَرَجِلِهِ. فَلَعَمْرِي لَقَدْ فَوَّقَ لَكُمْ سَهْمَ الْوَعِيدِ، وَأَغْرَقَ لَكُم بِالنَّزْعِ الشَّدِيدِ، وَرَمَاكُمْ مِنْ مَكَان قَرِيب، و (قَالَ رَبِّ بِمَا أَغْوَيْتَنِي لأَزَيِّنَنَّ لَهُمْ فِي الأَرْضِ وَلأَغْوِيَنَّهُمْ أَجْمَعِينَ)

Sermon 1: The Holy Quran and Sunnah

The Holy Prophet Muhammad
(peace be upin him and his family),

like other Prophets left us, a book so that we have a guide. All Prophets leave us instructions with important information that we need to know. The Holy Quran is what the Prophet Muhammad left us. It has lots of information about what to do, what we shouldnt do. It tells us what is good for us and what is bad for us and it has lots of lessons and stories within it.

But the Prophet left among you the same which other Prophets left among their peoples, because Prophets do not leave them unattended (in the dark) without a clear path and a standing ensign, namely the book of your Creator clarifying its permission and prohibitions, its obligations and discretion, its repealing in junctions and the repealed ones, its permissible matters and compulsory ones, its particulars and the general ones, its lessons and illustrations, its long and the short ones, its clear and obscure ones, detailing its abbreviations and clarifying its obscurities.

وَخَلَّفَ فِيكُمْ مَا خَلَّفَتِ الْأَنْبِيَاءُ فِي أُمَمِها، إِذْ لَم يَتْرُكُوهُمْ هَمَلاً،

بِغَيْرِ طَرِيق واضِح، ولاَعَلَمٍ قَائِم.

كِتَابَ رَبِّكُمْ [فِيكُمْ:] مُبَيِّناً حَلاَلَهُ وَحَرامَهُ، وَفَرَائِضَهُ وَفَضَائِلَهُ،

وَنَاسِخَهُ وَمَنْسُوخَهُ، وَرُخَصَهُ وَعَزَائِمَهُ، وَخَاصَّهُ وَعَامَّهُ،

وَعِبَرَهُ وَأَمْثَالَهُ، وَمُرْسَلَهُ وَمَحْدُودَهُ، وَمُحْكَمَهُ وَمُتَشَابِهَهُ، مُفَسِّراً

جُمَلَهُ، وَمُبَيِّناً غَوَامِضَهُ.

THE HOLY QURAN

Made Easy for Kids
Vol. 1, Surah 1-10

Available at Amazon in paperback
and on kindle versions.

safoopublications.com

I am Salah

Amal Al-Aride
Kasim Al-Janabi

Shia Edition

I am Ghadeer

Safoo Publications

I am Karbala

Safoo Publications

Find more books to read at

safoopublications.com

Available at Amazon in paperback
and on kindle versions.

Made in the USA
Middletown, DE
18 February 2023

25180584R00015